WRITERS IN BRITAIN

The Romantic Poets

Nicola Barber and P

The SIC

O Rose thou a
The invisible wo
That flies in the
In the howling storm:

Has found out thy bed
Of crimson joy:
And his dark secret love
Does thy life destroy.

Published by Evans Brothers Limited
2A Portman Mansions
Chiltern Street
London W1M 1LE

© Evans Brothers Limited 2000

First published 2000

Printed at Oriental Press ,Dubai,U.A.E.

British Cataloguing in Publication Data

Barber, Nicola
    The romantic poets. - (Writers in Britain)
    1. Poets, English – 19th century - Biography - Juvenile
literature
    1. Title II. Lee-Browne, Patrick
    821.7'09145

    ISBN 0237521180

Acknowledgements

Consultant – Marion Thain, Lecturer in English Literature at The University of Birmingham

Editor – Victoria Brooker
Designer – Ann Samuel
Production – Jenny Mulvanny

For permission to reproduce copyright material, the authors and publishers gratefully acknowledge the following:

Cover (left) Fitzwilliam Museum, University of Cambridge/Bridgeman Art Library (top right) Collections/Liz Stares (bottom right) Birmingham Museums and Art Gallery/Bridgeman Art Library title page Fitzwilliam Museum, University of Cambridge **page 3** Roy Rainford/Robert Harding Picture Library **page 6** Library of Congress, Washington D.C/Bridgeman Art Library **page 7** (top) Mary Evans Picture Library (bottom) Royal Albert Memorial Museum, Exeter/Bridgeman Art Library **page 8** (top right) Private Collection/Bridgeman Art Library (top left) Private Collection/Bridgeman Art Library (bottom) Mary EvansPicture Library **page 9** Royal Agricultural Society of England, Stoneleigh/Bridgeman Art Library **page 10** Fitzwilliam Museum, University of Cambridge/Bridgeman Art Library **page 11** (top) Fitzwilliam Museum, University of Cambridge (bottom) Fitzwilliam Museum, University of Cambridge **page 12** (top) Guildhall Library, Corporation of London/Bridgeman Art Library (bottom) South African National Gallery, Cape Town, South Africa/Bridgeman Art Library **page 13** (top) Private Collection/Bridgeman Art Library (bottom) British Library **page 14** (top) Private Collection/Bridgeman Art Library (bottom) The Wordsworth Trust **page 15** British Museum/Bridgeman Art Library (inset) Jean Brooks/Robert Harding Picture Library **page 16** (top) Collections/Liz Stares (bottom) Dove Cottage Trust, Grasmere/Bridgeman Art Library **page 17** Roy Rainford/Robert Harding Picture Library **page 18** Robert Harding Picture Library **page 19** (top) Victoria & Albert Museum/Bridgeman Art Library (bottom) Mary Evans Picture Library **page 20** (top) Robert Harding Picture Library (bottom) Private Collection/Bridgeman Art Library **page 21** (middle) Mary Evans Picture Library (bottom) Walker Art Gallery, Liverpool/Bridgeman Art Library **page 22** Fitzwilliam Museum, University of Cambridge/Bridgeman Art Library **page 23** (top) Fitzwilliam Museum, University of Cambridge/Bridgeman Art Library (bottom) Guildhall Art Gallery, Corporation of London **page 24** Prado, Madrid/Bridgeman Art Library page 25 (top) Birmingham Museums and Art Gallery/Bridgeman Art Library (bottom) Mary Evans Picture Library **page 26** The Makins Collection/Bridgeman Art Library **page 27** (top) Mary Evans Picture Library (bottom) Aquarius Picture Library

Contents

Historical background

The poets' lives

The Romantic period

A time of revolution

A popular figure

John Wilkes was a journalist and MP who wrote newspaper articles which strongly criticised King George III and his minister, the Earl of Bute. In 1763 Wilkes was imprisoned under an old law which allowed the authorities to arrest someone for a political offence without having to identify them. Wilkes successfully challenged the legality of this action, and became a popular figure of resistance to the power of the king and his court.

The six English poets described in this book are often referred to as 'Romantic' poets, or even *the* Romantic poets. Used in this way the term 'Romantic' indicates that these poets shared similar ideas about the purpose, the subject matter and style of their poetry. It also links them to a wider way of thinking and writing that swept through Britain and Europe towards the end of the 18th century. The Romantic movement was strongest in Britain from around 1790 until 1830, but its influence can be seen in many of the major writers of the 19th and 20th centuries, in novels and drama as well as poetry.

The second half of the 18th century, in which each of these poets was born, was a time of great change and uncertainty. In the 17th century King Charles I had been beheaded by order of Parliament and James II forced by Parliament's actions to surrender the throne to William of Orange and his wife Mary. Although in the 18th century the monarchy retained much political power, it was still possible for strong-minded individuals to challenge the King through the courts and through Parliament (see box).

Down with the monarchy!

In Europe and America, clashes between people and the monarchy took a more violent and long-lasting form than in Britain. The inhabitants of the 13 British colonies on the east coast of America were required to obey British laws and pay tax to Britain, yet they had no representatives in Parliament. Their dissatisfaction at the government's refusal to consider their case led to the publication of the Declaration of Rights in Philadelphia in 1774. The following year the American War of Independence broke out, which lasted until 1783. In 1776 the Congress of the American colonies adopted the Declaration of Independence, which became the legal basis of the new United States of America.

Signing the American Declaration of Independence on 4 July 1776. It was drafted by Thomas Jefferson and stated that 'all men are created equal'.

The French Revolution erupted out of similar popular discontent. Although in France there was a parliament to represent the people, it had not met since 1614, which allowed the monarch and the aristocracy to keep power very firmly to themselves. In 1789, encouraged by the example of the American colonists, parliament formed a new National Assembly. When the

The French king, Louis XVI, was executed by the guillotine in January 1793. The guillotine was a device with a sharp blade that cut off the head of its victims. It was used to kill thousands of people during the French Revolution.

French king, Louis XVI, threatened armed force to prevent this, the people of Paris revolted and attacked the Bastille, an old prison in the city, on 14 July 1789. The mood of revolution quickly spread throughout the rest of the country. As in America, a Declaration of the Rights of Man was issued by the Assembly, but it was not until 1792 that a republic was declared. In the course of the wars against other European nations that followed the French Revolution, a young general called Napoleon Bonaparte rose to power. After seizing control of the country in 1799, he crowned himself emperor in 1804 and the Republic came to an end.

Opposing views

The revolutions in France and America provoked much alarm and public debate in Britain. The politician Edmund Burke (right) was in favour of giving more freedom to America after the War of Independence broke out but, in 1790, his *Reflections on the Revolution in France* argued against the people taking the law into their own hands. Thomas Paine, an Englishman who had helped the Americans to win independence, replied with *The Rights of Man* (1791-2) which claimed that revolution was a justified way of removing deep-rooted tyranny.

Social and cultural change

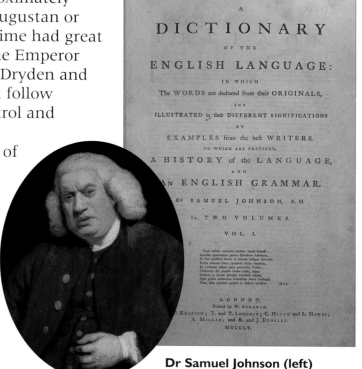

The period in English literature from approximately 1660 to 1780 is often referred to as the Augustan or Neo-Classical age because the writers of that time had great respect for the Latin writers from the age of the Emperor Augustus (27 BC–AD 14). Authors such as John Dryden and Alexander Pope believed that literature should follow careful rules, which imitated the balance, control and order of the Classical authors. *The Dictionary*, compiled by Dr Samuel Johnson, was the first of its kind in English, and is typical of the desire of many thinkers at the time to organise and control language.

However, not everyone felt so settled: the American and French revolutions (see pages 6–7) were part of wider changes in social and economic life which brought increased prosperity for some people, but misery and hardship for many more. The Agricultural and Industrial revolutions (see page 9) drove many people away from rural areas to the expanding industrial cities. The appalling conditions endured by labourers in both town and country, and the feeling that greed and the desire for profit were gradually wearing away at decent human values, moved many writers.

Dr Samuel Johnson (left) compiled the first dictionary of the English language, published in 1755.

A slum scene in London in the 1870s. Many people in the industrial cities of the 19th century lived in overcrowded and insanitary conditions.

William Godwin, for example, argued in *An Enquiry concerning Political Justice* (1793) that people should arrange themselves in small self-sufficient communities, in which the needs of individuals would be met far more effectively than by corrupt national government. In *Rural Rides* (1830) the political journalist William Cobbett exposed the injustices done to the workers in the countryside in the name of progress. One incident in the book describes how agricultural workers were driven to mending roads to earn money because the farmers were too poor

to employ them. Yet the money to pay for road-mending came out of taxes collected from those same poor farmers:

> 66 *It is odd enough, too, that the parish roads should become* better *and better as the farmers become* poorer *and poorer! …Yes, this country now contains a body of occupiers of the land, who suffer the land to go to decay for* want of means to pay a sufficiency of labourers; *and at the same time, are* compelled to pay those labourers for doing that which is of no use to the occupiers! 99
>
> Rural Rides

Economic revolutions

The change in farming methods known as the Agricultural Revolution was prompted by the need for more efficient production of food for a growing population. The land had traditionally been farmed in small plots, which gave ownership or employment to many, but this did not make economic sense. So gradually the wealthier farmers bought out the poorer ones. Areas of common land, where villagers had the right to graze their animals, were absorbed into the larger estates in a process known as enclosure. These developments were matched with the invention of machinery such as Jethro Tull's seed drill, and improvements to the methods of rotating and fertilising crops. The reduced need for farm labour coincided with the Industrial Revolution, which saw manufacturing move out of people's own homes into large mills and factories. For example, the invention of new machines that allowed thread and cloth to be produced more efficiently revolutionised the textile industry. Improvements in the manufacture of iron and steel made it possible to create more sophisticated industrial machinery, as well as structures such as bridges and railways.

A meeting of farmers to examine the latest agricultural machinery. The picture was painted in the 1840s.

William Blake (1757–1827)

This portrait of William Blake was painted in 1821, when he was in the last years of his life.

William Blake was the earliest of the major Romantic poets, using his poetry to combine politics with literature in a new and distinctive style. Blake was born in 1757, the second son of a London hosier. He grew up in easy-going but simple circumstances with three brothers and a sister, and from an early age he showed talent as an artist. On finishing his education he took up a career as an engraver, which he followed throughout his life. As an apprentice he was sent to sketch the tombs in Westminster Abbey, which inspired a lifelong love of Gothic and medieval art. For his designs he was also particularly attracted to scenes from the Bible, and to the poetry of the medieval Italian poet Dante Alighieri (1265-1321) and John Milton (1608-74).

A loving couple

At the age of 24 Blake met and fell in love with Catherine Boutcher, the daughter of a market-gardener, and they married a year later. Catherine was a strong and loving wife, who became an artist and engraver in her own right. A friend described them in the following terms:

> 66 *She…is so truly the Half of her good Man, that they seem animated by one Soul, & that a soul of indefatigable Industry and Benevolence.* 99

Apart from a period of three years (1800–03) spent in Felpham, Sussex, Blake lived the whole of his life in London, and it was a largely uneventful one on the outside. But he was a man of extraordinary energy and imagination. He joined a circle of young talented artists such as John Flaxman and Henry Fuseli, and met radical thinkers including Thomas Paine (see page 7), William Godwin (see page 8) and his wife Mary Wollstonecraft (see pages 20 and 27). During the French Revolution, Blake wore a red cap in the streets in support of the republican cause.

A man of vision

At the age of eight, Blake saw his first vision. It was a tree on Peckham Rye, in London, filled with angels. Another time he saw angels walking among hay-makers in the meadows. At the age of 15, Blake was interviewed by an engraver named Rylands, of whom he said, 'It looks as if he will live to be hanged.' Twelve years later, Rylands was hanged for forgery. When Blake's brother Robert died of tuberculosis at the age of 19, Blake (who had nursed him through his last illness) saw Robert's soul rise through the ceiling, 'clapping its hands for joy'.

Blake the poet

Blake was a poet just as much as an artist. He wrote about his political and religious beliefs in a number of long and highly complex poems such as *The French Revolution* (1791), *America; A Prophecy* (1793) and *The Marriage of Heaven and Hell* (1793). He illustrated many of his poems, and the most well-known of these were published in the collection called *Songs of Innocence and Experience* (1794). Blake claimed that his dead brother Robert (see box) taught him in a vision a particular method of engraving which allowed him to hand-colour the finished design as if it were a drawing. The *Songs of Innocence and Experience* are a remarkable combination of art and words, in which the simplicity of the poetry and artwork combine to express the depth of Blake's feeling about the joys and dangers facing young children in the modern world.

Blake believed that his illustrations for the *Songs of Innocence and Experience* were as important as the poems.

> *O Rose thou art sick.*
> *The invisible worm*
> *That flies in the night*
> *In the howling storm*
>
> *Has found out thy bed*
> *Of crimson joy:*
> *And his dark secret love*
> *Does thy life destroy.*

'The Sick Rose'

Blake found it hard to make a living as an engraver and poet, and much of the middle part of his life was spent with little recognition of his talents. In his last years, he enjoyed better fortune, and his paintings illustrating the story of Job from the Bible are perhaps his greatest achievement. He died at the age of 69, singing hymns of joy on his deathbed, and was buried in Bunhill Fields, London.

'There were not found Women fair as the Daughters of Job in all the Land...' One of Blake's illustrations for the *Book of Job*, published in 1825.

Samuel Taylor Coleridge (1772–1834)

Coleridge attended school at Christ's Hospital in London from 1782-91.

Robert Southey (1774-1843) was a poet and friend of Coleridge. Southey became Poet Laureate in 1813.

Samuel Taylor Coleridge was the youngest of ten children of the Reverend John Coleridge and his wife, Anne Bowden. He was born on 21 October 1772 at Ottery St Mary, Devon, where his father was both vicar of the parish church and headmaster of the local school. As the youngest child in a large and talented family, Coleridge had to fight for attention, but his father (whom he adored) died when he was only nine. The young Coleridge was sent to a boarding school, Christ's Hospital, in the City of London. From there he won a scholarship to Cambridge University in 1791, where he studied mathematics and classics.

In 1794 he met Robert Southey, who was proposing to emigrate to America and set up a small community in order to escape the pressures of British society. Coleridge was drawn into Southey's plans, and instead of completing his degree at Cambridge, he moved to Bristol where he established himself as a political speaker and writer, enthusiastically supporting many of the ideals of the French Revolution (see page 7). In October 1795, with Southey's encouragement, Coleridge married Sara Fricker, the sister of Southey's wife. But shortly after the wedding, Southey abandoned his plans for the American venture, which cast a long shadow over the couple's happiness.

A military interlude

While Coleridge was at Cambridge, he found it hard to avoid getting into debt. Although his brother George frequently bailed him out, in December 1793 Coleridge tried an alternative means of supporting himself. He allowed himself to be recruited into the 15th Light Dragoons, under the false name of Silas Tomkyn Comberbache. This was not a success, since Coleridge knew nothing about horses, and was not at all suited to military life. Another of his brothers was a successful soldier who helped to have him discharged from the army, on the grounds of insanity!

Coleridge and Wordsworth

It was at this time that Coleridge met William Wordsworth (see page 14), and in the course of the next three years the two poets shared ideas and thoughts that allowed the creative talents of both men to grow. They developed a partnership which culminated in the publication of *Lyrical Ballads* (1798), an important landmark in the Romantic movement. Wordsworth and Coleridge chose characters and settings for their poems that expressed a different view of life from that normally written about in the poetry of the time. Coleridge contributed four poems to the book, including 'The Rime of the Ancient Mariner' and 'Kubla Khan' (see box), while the rest of the poems in it were by Wordsworth. At first, *Lyrical Ballads* was badly received by some critics, including Coleridge's former friend Southey.

The friendship with Wordsworth and his sister Dorothy lasted for many years. However, Coleridge became infatuated with Sara Hutchinson, Wordsworth's sister-in-law, and separated from his own wife to live by himself. At this point he also abandoned responsibility for his three children, and it was in fact Robert Southey who took charge of their welfare. As Coleridge grew older he was afflicted by a growing sense of having failed to fulfil his potential, which was made worse by an increasing dependency on opium and alcohol. After 1802 he found it difficult to write poetry. He spent his later years in London lecturing, writing a highly individual biography, *Biographia Literaria* (1817), and publishing a final collection of the poems written earlier in his career.

Coleridge is often viewed as a poet and writer who promised more than he ever actually delivered. He developed a particular voice in poetry, referred to as 'conversational', but he produced relatively few real masterpieces.

This portrait of Samuel Taylor Coleridge was painted when the poet was in his 40s. In 1810, he quarrelled with Wordsworth, and the two men were never entirely reconciled.

Coleridge's poem 'Kubla Khan' opens with the words:
'In Xanadu did Kubla Khan A stately pleasure dome decree...'

The person from Porlock

One of the most well-known poems in English has a strange story attached to it. Coleridge composed 'Kubla Khan' while in a trance under the influence of opium, which he took as a pain-killer. Coleridge claimed that he woke from unconsciousness and was in the process of writing down the poem when he was interrupted for an hour by 'a person on business from Porlock' (a nearby town). When he was finally free to remember the rest of the poem, it had slipped from his memory. As a result only a fragment of the whole survived, although the truth of the story has never been proved.

William Wordsworth (1770–1850)

Illiam Wordsworth was born in 1770 in Cockermouth, on the edge of the Lake District in northwest England. His home life was not particularly happy – his mother died when he was eight and his father when he was 13 – but he enjoyed his time boarding at Hawkshead grammar school from the ages of nine to 17. It was during this period that he began to appreciate the power and value of nature which was to provide the subject matter of so much of his poetry.

> " ...even then I felt
> Gleams like the flashing of a shield; – the earth
> And common face of Nature spake to me
> Rememberable things. "
>
> The Prelude Book 1

A portrait of William Wordsworth set against the landscape of the Lake District that he loved.

Hawkshead school had an excellent academic record, and Wordsworth went from there to Cambridge in 1787. The university failed to inspire him, however, and although a career in the church or the law was the likely outcome of his studies, when he left Cambridge in 1791 he decided to delay making a decision and went instead to France. This was a major turning-point in his life.

Revolutionary fervour

France in 1791-2 was in revolutionary turmoil (see page 7). Wordsworth was caught up in the heady atmosphere of political and intellectual freedom, and his experiences in France had a lasting effect on him. For several years afterwards he led an unsettled life. He toured the West Country on foot, stayed with his sister Dorothy (with whom he spent all his adult life) in the Lake District, and lived in London, where he met and talked with William Godwin (see page 8). In Bristol, in the late summer of 1795, he met Coleridge for the first time. The next four years were another period of great significance, for during that time Wordsworth and Coleridge discussed politics and art, and shared ideas for a style of poetry which came to fruition in *Lyrical Ballads* (see page 13).

This silhouette of Dorothy Wordsworth hangs in Dove Cottage, Grasmere, the Wordsworths' home from 1799 to 1808.

Wordsworth and nature

While *Lyrical Ballads* was being prepared
for printing in July 1798, Wordsworth
went on another walking tour, this time
in the Wye Valley on the border of England
and Wales. There he wrote 'Lines Written
a few miles above Tintern Abbey', a poem
which sums up his feelings at that time
about the relationship between Nature and
human nature. The poem was included in
Lyrical Ballads, and stands as the last piece
in the book.

Wordsworth believed that Nature existed
as a force in its own right, and that it had
a positive effect on people's behaviour
and feelings:

> 		...such, perhaps,
> As may have had no trivial influence
> On that best portion of a good man's life;
> His little, nameless, unremembered acts
> Of kindness and of love.

**This painting of Tintern Abbey by the English
artist JMW Turner captures the remote beauty
of the ruins, unchanged today (see above left).
Wordsworth was inspired by the peaceful
atmosphere of the place.**

Just at the time when *Lyrical Ballads* was
appearing to mixed reviews in the bookshops, the
Wordsworths and Coleridge set off for Germany.
This brief visit of nine months, during which
Wordsworth started work on *The Prelude* (see box
on page 17), was followed by a long period of
stability when William and Dorothy moved to the
Lake District. They lived at Dove Cottage, Grasmere
and later at Rydal Mount, Ambleside. It was in the
Lake District that Wordsworth truly set down his
roots and established himself as the leading figure
of the Romantic movement.

Annette Vallon

During his time in France, Wordsworth met
and fell in love with Annette Vallon. She gave
birth to a daughter, Caroline Wordsworth, in
December 1792, but Wordsworth had
returned to England by the end of the month
without seeing his daughter. He never
married Annette, although they were to
meet several times again. The first of these
occasions was in 1802, when he also met
Caroline, then aged nine, for the first time.

Wordsworth's later years

When he moved to Dove Cottage in 1799 Wordsworth felt that he had arrived home, 'a termination and a last retreat', as he called it in one poem. He continued to tour, visiting Scotland, Wales and Europe on various occasions throughout the next 50 years, and in 1802 he married Mary Hutchinson, a fellow Lakelander whom he had known since childhood. The marriage was a happy one, though Mary was soon preoccupied with raising and managing their large family. His sister Dorothy, always his closest companion, remained his inspiration and intellectual partner.

Fame and success came slowly but steadily in the next 50 years. Perhaps the bleakest period in his life was in the mid-1830s, when Dorothy developed a form of senile dementia, and his wife's sister Sara died, as did Coleridge and a number of Wordsworth's close friends from school and university. But still he survived. In 1843, he was created Poet Laureate, though on the understanding that he would not be required to write anything. As he died, on Shakespeare's birthday, 23 April 1850, the cuckoo-clock in the room called out that it was noon.

Dove Cottage, in Grasmere, stands in the centre of the Lake District. Today, the cottage is kept in a similar condition to when the Wordsworths lived there.

William and Mary Wordsworth, painted in 1839. Mary survived her husband by nine years.

Wordsworth's poetry

The poetry for which Wordsworth is best remembered is often concerned with nature. 'To Daffodils', which begins:
   'I wandered lonely as a cloud
   That floats on high o'er vales and hills'
is perhaps the most well-known of his works. But Wordsworth was always keenly interested in the relationship between people and their surroundings; his poetry is often about the rural poor and the dignity that their difficult circumstances bring them. A chance meeting with a beggar or a reaper or a leech-gatherer sparked questions or gave

pause for thought. In his large-scale work, such as *The Prelude* or his unfinished poem *The Recluse,* he explored the effect of people and places on his own mind and attitudes as a poet.

In his autobiographical poem *The Prelude* (see box below) Wordsworth describes how one day he and a friend passed a starving country girl knitting while leading a cow:

> ...at the sight my friend
> In agitation said, "Tis against that
> That we are fighting," I with him believed
> That... poverty
> Abject as this would in a little time
> Be found no more. ... 99

Wordsworth's writing is often very visual, set frequently in the Lake District, or in places he visited such as the Scottish highlands or the Alps. For the most part it is truthful, rather than visionary, recording things that actually happened or thoughts he felt in response to events.

> 66 The music in my heart I bore
> Long after it was heard no more. 99
> The Solitary Reaper

Poetical intentions

In a preface to the second edition of *Lyrical Ballads,* published in 1802, Wordsworth explained the thinking behind the book. He wrote that he had aimed 'to choose incidents and situations from common life and to relate or describe them...in a selection of language really used by men, ...tracing in them...the primary laws of our nature.' In the same preface he described poetry as 'the spontaneous overflow of powerful feelings; it takes its origin from emotion recollected in tranquillity.'

Rydal Water in the Lake District. The scenery of the Lake District and the lives of its inhabitants were a constant source of inspiration for Wordsworth.

The growth of the poet's mind

Over the course of 50 years Wordsworth worked on a long poem, addressed to Coleridge, tracing his own life from early childhood up to his return to Grasmere in 1799. The first version was 978 lines long. Within the next six years it had grown to five books, and by 1805 the poem was 13 books long. Mary Wordsworth gave the poem its title, *The Prelude,* when it was published after Wordsworth's death in 1850. By then it had reached its final form of 14 books. Although Wordsworth and Coleridge had grown apart in the later years of Coleridge's life, the final version remained addressed to Wordsworth's old friend.

George Gordon, Lord Byron (1788–1824)

*T*he remaining three writers in this book – Byron, Shelley and Keats – represent a 'second generation' of Romantic poets, growing up after the French Revolution, dying young and, in the case of Byron and Shelley, living a far more flamboyant and unsettled lifestyle than their older counterparts.

Newstead Abbey in Nottinghamshire. The house was given to the Byron family by King Henry VIII.

Byron's daughters

Byron had one daughter by his wife Annabella. Augusta Ada Byron (1815-1852) was a brilliant mathematician who carried out early research into cybernetics and electricity. In the 1840s she worked with Charles Babbage in the development of the first computer. She tried to use her theories to ensure success on the racecourse, but ran up huge gambling debts.

While Byron was living in Geneva, he renewed an affair with Mary Jane, or 'Claire' Clairmont (the step-daughter of William Godwin). She gave birth to a daughter, Allegra, in 1817. But neither she nor Byron had any time for their luckless daughter: Allegra was sent to a convent near Ravenna, where she died at the age of five.

George Gordon Byron was the son of a dashing and extravagant soldier, known as 'Mad Jack' Byron and a Scots heiress, Catherine Gordon. He was brought up in Scotland by his mother, his father having died when he was three. At the age of ten he unexpectedly inherited the family title, becoming the 6th Baron Byron, and taking possession of the family estates at Newstead Abbey in Nottinghamshire. He was educated at Harrow School and Cambridge University, where he published his first collection of poetry, wasted a good deal of money and had a number of brief but passionate love affairs.

Byron's first major poetic achievement was *Childe Harold's Pilgrimage*, a poem based on his travels around Europe from 1809 to 1811. The work was an immediate success and, as a result, Byron enjoyed the attentions of London society. This led him into affairs with, among others, Lady Caroline Lamb, (the wife of the future prime minister, Lord Melbourne) and his own (married) half-sister, Augusta Byron. Although Byron married Annabella Milbanke in 1815, the marriage was never a strong one, and the couple were legally separated a year later. Byron's earlier immorality had been tolerated while he was on a wave of popularity, but opinion turned against him and in April 1816 he left Britain, never to return.

Byron abroad

Byron lived in Geneva and various Italian cities including Venice, Ravenna and Pisa, having a number of new love affairs, including one with the stepdaughter of William Godwin (see box on page 18). While living in Venice, Byron started work on his most substantial poem, *Don Juan*, which was still unfinished at his death.

In 1820 Byron joined a secret political movement dedicated to freeing Italy from its Austrian rulers. His interest in revolutionary politics led him to sail to Greece in 1823 to support the War of Independence that Greek patriots had started against the Turks. He tried to unite the various factions among the Greek forces, but he contracted a fever in the spring of 1824 and died on April 19. He was mourned as a political and military hero and buried back in England, in the family vault.

Byron's extraordinary and complex character is reflected in the variety and energy of his writing. Sometimes his poetry is tender and sensitive, at other times confident and triumphant and yet again cynical and self-mocking. Like Wordsworth, he often made himself and his experiences the subject of his poetry, which is recognised as one of the main characteristics of Romantic poetry.

The Grand Canal in Venice, portrayed by the English painter JMW Turner in 1840. Byron first visited the city in 1817.

Byron is shown here in the costume of a Greek patriot. He died in 1824 while fighting for the Greek cause.

> 66 *So, we'll go no more a roving*
> *So late into the night,*
> *Though the heart be still as loving,*
> *And the moon be still as bright.* 99

An ear for music

Byron had a gift for writing strong, emotional poetry. His work often relies on rhythm for its effect, as in 'The Destruction of Sennacherib':

> 66 *The Assyrian came down like the wolf on the fold,*
> *And his cohorts were gleaming in purple and gold;*
> *And the sheen of their spears was like stars on the sea,*
> *When the blue wave rolls nightly on deep Gallilee.* 99

Percy Bysshe Shelley (1792–1822)

Eton College, Berkshire. Shelley attended the school from 1804 to 1810.

The love affair between Shelley and Mary Godwin (shown here) shocked Shelley's family and friends.

The poetry of Percy Bysshe Shelley was perhaps the most obviously political of the six major Romantic poets, although much of his political poetry is not widely read today.

Shelley was, like Byron, a member of a long-established and well-connected family. He was born at Field Place, in Sussex and, as the eldest son of his parents Timothy and Elizabeth Shelley, stood to inherit the family fortune. But from an early age, Percy Shelley refused to conform. He went to Eton College, where he quickly made a name for himself by refusing to 'fag' (do menial tasks) for the senior boys. There is also a story that he electrocuted one of the teachers by setting a booby-trap on the door-handle of his study.

While he was still at school he published two novels and two volumes of poetry. The quality of this writing was not great, but it shows the young Shelley's energy and ambition to establish himself as a writer. In 1810 he went to Oxford, but he was expelled from the university in March 1811 for publishing a pamphlet called *The Necessity of Atheism*, which challenged traditional ideas about God's existence.

Scandal

Having left Oxford, Shelley spent a short time at home in Field Place, but in August 1811 he further upset his family by running away with Harriet Westbrook, the daughter of a well-to-do coffee-house owner, and marrying her in Edinburgh. He was 19; she was 16. Shelley's father and grandfather were horrified, and tried to force him to return to Sussex. Instead he, Harriet and her sister Eliza travelled to the Lake District, where they met Robert Southey (see page 12). The next two years saw the Shelleys living in Dublin (where Shelley planned to launch a political movement to rescue the Irish peasantry from their misery and poverty), North Wales, Devon, and London. It was in London that Shelley arranged an introduction to William Godwin (see page 8). Godwin had a daughter called Mary by his first wife, Mary Wollstonecraft (see page 27), and, in 1814, Shelley eloped with

Mary Godwin. Together with her stepsister Claire Clairmont (see page 18) they went to the Continent.

At first, Godwin and many other of Shelley's friends were horrified by this action. But, by 1815, Shelley had patched up some of the differences with his father, and settled with Mary and Claire near Eton. By this stage Shelley had two children by his wife Harriet, and Mary gave birth to a son in January 1816. In April of that year Shelley, Mary and Claire moved to Geneva. There Claire revived her affair with Byron, who had left England for good (see page 18) and the two men shared ideas about poetry and writing.

Tragedy struck soon afterwards. Mary Godwin's step-sister, Fanny, and Harriet Shelley both committed suicide at the end of 1816. Returning to England, Shelley made an unsuccessful claim for custody of their two children and married Mary Godwin. Frustrated with English society, Shelley, Mary and Claire left for Italy in March 1818; he was never to return to England. This final period spent in Italy was productive and frustrating by turns, and tragedy returned when both of his children by Mary died through illness. Shelley and Byron developed an interest in sailing, and it was while on his boat that Shelley was drowned in an accident still shrouded in mystery. In his pocket was a copy of the poems of John Keats.

> 66 *Drive my dead thoughts over the universe*
> *Like withered leaves to quicken a new birth;*
> *And, by the incantation of this verse,*
> *Scatter, as from an unextinguished hearth*
> *Ashes and sparks, my words among mankind!* 99
>
> Ode to the West Wind

A Productive Party

While Shelley and Byron were living in Geneva they often discussed the contemporary fascination with Gothic ghost stories and tales of the supernatural. Mary Godwin would listen and join in. One night, after they had been talking about the revival of the dead and the creation of life from inert matter, she dreamt up the bones of a short story which was to become the novel *Frankenstein*.

An early illustration for Mary Shelley's *Frankenstein*

A romantic end

The story of Shelley's death and burial is a highly dramatic one. On 8 July 1822 he was drowned while at sea in his boat, the *Don Juan*. His body was washed ashore several days later and buried where it was found. On 15 August Byron and two other friends of Shelley (Leigh Hunt and Edward Trelawny) dug up the grave, built a funeral pyre and burnt the body on the beach. Byron, overcome with emotion, swam out to his own boat, the *Bolivar*, which was anchored offshore, while Trelawny snatched Shelley's heart out of the fire.

Shelley's funeral pyre, as imagined by the artist Louis Fournier. The figure standing slightly apart from the others is Byron.

John Keats (1795–1821)

This portrait of Keats was painted in about 1818 by his friend Joseph Severn. Severn accompanied Keats to Rome in 1820 and nursed him through his final sickness.

The last of these Romantic poets, John Keats, was the first to die. Like Wordsworth and Coleridge, he lost his parents early – his father died when he was nine and his mother when he was 15 – but his childhood was in many ways a happy and fulfilled one.

Keats was born and brought up in London, and during his time at boarding school in Enfield he made many friends and impressed them with his equal interest in fighting and writing. His mother's death in 1810 laid an early responsibility on him to earn a living and so at the age of fifteen he was apprenticed to a surgeon, which in those days was a career less highly thought of than a doctor. He went on to study at Guy's and St Thomas's hospitals and in July 1816 he qualified as a surgeon and apothecary (a profession similar to a modern-day chemist). However, throughout his training Keats had showed as much enthusiasm for poetry as for medicine, and he had built up a close circle of friends that included the poet and essayist Leigh Hunt, the artists Benjamin Haydon and Joseph Severn, and the lawyer John Hamilton Reynolds.

In October 1816, when he became 21, Keats decided to give up his career in medicine and become a full-time poet. He had begun writing poetry in 1814, but he now set himself the task of composing a long poem to prove his talent. The result of this self-imposed test was 'Endymion', completed in 1817. An acquaintance with Percy Shelley, friendship with Leigh Hunt, a meeting with Wordsworth and other personal concerns such as the poor health of his brother, Tom, provided the motivation for other early poems.

Lulworth Cove

The story of the unfulfilled love between Keats and Fanny Brawne is very sad. It seems from his letters and journals that Keats linked his illness in 1819 and 1820 to his frustration over their relationship. Writing to his friend Charles Brown he wrote: 'I should have had her when I was in health, and I should have remained well.' At the start of the journey to Italy, the boat in which Keats was travelling stopped at Lulworth Cove, in Dorset, where Keats composed his last poem, a sonnet dedicated to Fanny Brawne, which begins:

66 *Bright star! would I were as steadfast as thou art –*
Not in lone splendour hung aloft the night. 99

A fruitful period

In 1817 Keats published his first collection of poetry, which was well received, and in the next year he went on a tour to the Lake District and Scotland, where he visited Fingal's Cave on the island of Staffa and climbed to the top of Ben Nevis. He was forced by a sore throat to return home in August. Back in London he found a number of negative reviews of his work and his brother Tom suffering seriously from tuberculosis. Tom died at the end of the year. But despite these misfortunes, Keats continued to write with great energy and increasing skill, and in September

1818 he started work on another long poem, 'Hyperion'. Some time during 1818 he met and fell in love with a close neighbour, Fanny Brawne, and they were probably engaged in the autumn of 1819. Keats by this stage was writing poetry of great quality, and 1819 was the most productive year of his short life – the time when when he wrote most of the poems for which he is now remembered: 'Ode to a Nightingale', 'The Eve of St Agnes', 'Ode on a Grecian Urn', 'La Belle Dame sans Merci' and 'To Autumn'.

Illness

Money worries and uncertainty about the direction of his relationship with Fanny Brawne (they never really made their feelings for one another public) made Keats extremely depressed. His black mood was made worse by the realisation at the beginning of 1820 that he, too, was suffering from tuberculosis. Shelley invited him to stay in Pisa where the warm climate would aid recovery. Keats did not take up this offer, but he did arrange to travel to Rome with his friend Joseph Severn. The journey was a long and uncomfortable one, and by the time they arrived in Italy, Keats was in a bad state. His condition only got worse, and in February 1821, at the age of 25 and with just three published volumes of poetry to his name, he died.

> 66 *Darkling I listen; and for many a time*
> *I have been half in love with easeful Death…*
> *Now more than ever seems it rich to die,*
> *To cease upon the midnight with no pain.* 99
>
> Ode to a Nightingale

The manuscript of 'Ode to a Nightingale', written in 1819. Some of Keats's alterations are clearly visible. The poem begins: 'My heart aches and a drowsy numbness pains My sense, as though of hemlock I had drunk…'

A painter's poet

Keats found the inspiration for a number of his poems in medieval stories and Gothic art. Among the best known of these are 'Isabella' and 'The Eve of St Agnes'. These poems in turn provided the subject for famous paintings by Victorian painters such as Sir John Everett Millais, Holman Hunt and Arthur Hughes. Keats's ability to create a vivid scene in words made his poetry suitable for visual interpretation.

'The Eve of St Agnes' by William Holman Hunt

'Mind-forg'd manacles'

The Romantic poets and their world

The Romantic movement in literature coincided with a similar revolution in art. The Contintental painters Jacques Louis David and Francisco Goya were inspired by the political upheavals in France and Spain respectively, and many of their paintings depict the people and events of revolutionary Europe. In England William Blake, JMW Turner and John Constable were among the leading Romantic artists, but you have to look hard in their work to find evidence of the wars and revolutions that took place during their lifetimes. Blake presented his ideas in an abstract, non-literal way, while Turner and Constable were landscape artists, whose pictures take as their subject many of the key Romantic landmarks and landscapes such as Tintern Abbey (see page 15), the Alps and the Lake District.

'The Third of May, 1808' by Francisco Goya depicts the execution of a group of Spanish citizens by French troops after Napoleon's invasion of Spain in 1808. Goya uses dramatic contrasts of light and dark to give the painting great intensity.

Nature and the city

This focus on the landscape in the visual art of the period is partly a result of the influence of Wordsworth and the other 'Lake Poets' – including Coleridge and Southey – on artistic taste. The close association of landscape painting and the poetry of Wordsworth, in particular, means that the Romantic poets are often identified with Nature. Keats's 'Ode to a Nightingale' and 'To Autumn', and Wordsworth's 'To Daffodils' are among the most well-known poems in the language, as are Shelley's 'Ode to the West Wind' or 'To a Skylark'. All of these poems express the close link between poetic inspiration and the power of Nature.

However, a great deal of the Romantics' poetry is based very strongly in the city, too. Keats and Blake were both Londoners, and Byron and Shelley thrived on the company to be found in busy towns and cities.

Antique lands

Although Wordsworth believed strongly that poetry should be about real people in a real landscape, many familiar Romantic poems are set in the world of fantasy. Coleridge's 'Kubla Khan', for example, describes the 'stately pleasure dome' that is built for the great Mongol emperor Kubla Khan in Xanadu. Shelley's 'Ozymandias' conjures up the vision of a gigantic ruined statue standing alone in the desert of an 'antique land', while Keats's 'La Belle Dame Sans Merci' is about a knight who has been bewitched by a beautiful but cruel elf-maiden.

Blake's poem 'London' describes the misery and poverty on the capital's streets:

> In every cry of every man,
> In every infant's cry of fear,
> In every voice, in every ban,
> The mind-forg'd manacles I hear.
>
> How the chimney-sweeper's cry
> Every black'ning church appalls;
> And the hapless soldier's sigh
> Runs in blood down palace walls.

'Grasmere from the Rydal Road' by Francis Towne, painted in the same period as the Romantic poets were writing about the Lakes.

Politics was never far from the surface, either. Shelley's 'Mask of Anarchy' was written in response to the Peterloo massacre (see page 9) as an appeal to the working people of England to fight for their freedom against the tyranny of the government. In the poem Shelley included a vicious portrait of the Lord Chancellor, Lord Eldon, who had refused Shelley's request for custody of his children on the death of his wife (see page 21):

> His big tears, for he wept well,
> Turned to mill-stones as they fell.
>
> And the little children, who
> Round his feet played to and fro,
> Thinking every tear a gem,
> Had their brains knocked out by them.

Symbolic seascape

The Romantic poets wrote about things and places in a symbolic way to appeal the imagination of the reader. Samuel Taylor Coleridge used powerful symbols in his poem 'The Rime of the Ancient Mariner'. The poem recounts how the Mariner in a moment of stupidity shoots an albatross and has to endure a series of nightmarish experiences as a punishment. One important symbol is the sea, which represents, among other things, the open-ended vastness of each person's life, with all its possibilities and horrors; another is the albatross, which the other sailors hang around the Mariner's neck, and which symbolises the guilt and the responsibility resulting from his folly.

In this illustration by Gustav Doré for 'The Rime of the Ancient Mariner', the albatross settles on the ship as it sails through an icy sea.

The Romantic heritage

*A*s a major artistic movement, Romanticism has had a deep and lasting impact on writing and art from the early 19th century up to the present day. Even authors who deliberately write against the Romantic tradition, by doing so acknowledge its influence.

The poetic tradition

Of the six poets described in this book, it is perhaps Keats who left the strongest impression on the generations that followed him. Despite his relatively small output of poetry, much of which was written while he was still developing his talent, Keats's ability to recreate a sensual experience in the reader's imagination made his work particularly memorable. Besides the wealth of paintings that his poems inspired (see page 23), he also had a strong influence on Victorian poets such as Alfred Tennyson, Algernon Swinburne and Gerard Manley Hopkins and on modern ones such as Dylan Thomas.

'Mariana in the Moated Grange', painted in 1851 by Sir John Everett Millais. The picture illustrated a poem by Tennyson. Millais also painted scenes from Keats's poems.

The Byronic hero

One of the most enduring aspects of the Romantic period is the idea of the 'Byronic' hero. Byron became famous virtually overnight on the publication of *Childe Harold's Pilgrimage* in 1812 (see page 18). He had the advantages of a colourful background, plenty of charm, wit and vanity, and strikingly good looks. He was painted more often than any other poet of his generation, and his image

Mary Wollstonecraft

In 1792, Mary Wollstonecraft published *A Vindication of the Rights of Woman*. In it, she set out her ideas about women's rights, proposing that women should receive the same opportunities as men in education, politics and work. Wollstonecraft was part of a group of poets and thinkers that included William Godwin, Thomas Paine, Blake and Wordsworth. She married Godwin in 1797, but died soon after giving birth to their second daughter, Mary (see page 20).

A portrait of Mary Wollstonecraft. She visited France in 1792 to observe the effects of the French Revolution at first hand.

was used commercially in the same way that those of modern actors and celebrities are. Although he was rather over-weight and had a club foot, portraits and sculptures emphasise his handsome, brooding face and his artistic or exotic clothes. The mystique surrounding him was increased by his energetic social life and sexual magnetism, his political activities as a kind of freedom fighter, and his early death. This combination of romantic characteristics has persisted into the art forms of the modern age, particularly in films. For example, the middle name of the actor James Dean was Byron. After his death at the age of 24, Dean became a symbol of youthful rebellion and individuality, just like his earlier namesake.

The character of Heathcliff, from *Wuthering Heights*, is one example of a 'Byronic' hero. The author, Emily Brontë, was a keen reader of Byron's poetry.

'The unacknowledged legislators of the world'

The Romantic era was born out of the revolutionary beliefs and ideals of the end of the 18th century. In an essay called *The Defence of Poetry* Shelley claimed that poets were more in touch with the feelings and experiences of people than the politicians and rulers who governed them. In a famous phrase, he described poets as 'unacknowledged legislators of the world', meaning that they were the ones who established the true guidelines for people to follow. All of the poets described in this book believed passionately that the power of the imagination allows people to free themselves from the difficulties and restrictions of everyday life. For many modern-day readers, this is one of the greatest gifts passed down by the Romantic poets.

HISTORICAL EVENTS		ROMANTICS DATES
Dictionary compiled by Dr Samuel Johnson	**1755**	
	1756	William Godwin born
Repeal of the Corn Laws	**1757**	William Blake born
George III crowned king	**1760**	
	1770	William Wordsworth born
	1772	Samuel Taylor Coleridge born
Declaration of Rights in Philadelphia, America	**1774**	Robert Southey born
American War of Independence	**1775-83**	
Declaration of Independence in America	**1776**	
James Watts patents steam engine	**1782**	Blake marries Catherine Boutcher
George III becomes ill	**1788**	George Gordon Byron born
French Revolution starts with storming of Bastille, Paris, 14 July	**1789**	
Edmund Burke publishes *Reflections on the Revolution in France*	**1790**	
Thomas Paine replies with *The Rights of Man*	**1791-2**	Wordsworth travels in France
French republic is declared. Mary Wollstonecraft publishes *A Vindication of the Rights of Woman*	**1792**	Percy Bysshe Shelley born
	1794	Publication of *Songs of Innocence and Experience* by Blake. Coleridge meets Robert Southey.
	1795	Coleridge meets Wordsworth and marries Sara Fricker. John Keats born
	1798	Publication of first edition of *Lyrical Ballads* by Coleridge and Wordsworth. Byron becomes 6th Baron Byron.
Napoleon crowns himself emperor	**1799**	Wordsworth moves to Dove Cottage, Grasmere (until 1808)
	1800	Second edition of *Lyrical Ballads* published by Wordsworth
	1802	Wordsworth marries Mary Hutchinson
Battle of Trafalgar, 21 October	**1805**	
	1809-11	Byron travels in Europe
Prince of Wales appointed Prince Regent in place of George III	**1811**	Shelley marries Harriet Westbrook and meets Robert Southey

HISTORICAL EVENTS		ROMANTICS DATES
	1812	Byron publishes *Childe Harold's Pilgrimage*
	1813	Southey becomes Poet Laureate. Wordsworth and family settle at Rydal Mount in the Lake District
George Stephenson invents first locomotive	**1814**	Shelley elopes with Mary Godwin and goes to the Continent.
Battle of Waterloo, 18 June; Napoleon is sent into exile. Corn Law passed by British Parliament to protect price of wheat	**1815**	Byron marries Annabella Milbanke
	1816	Keats qualifies as a surgeon and decides to become a full-time poet. Byron separates from wife and leaves Britain, never to return
	1817	Keats completes 'Endymion' and publishes first collection of poetry *Literaria Biographia* published by Coleridge
	1818	Keats meets Fanny Brawne; his brother Tom dies of tuberculosis. Mary Shelley publishes *Frankenstein*
Peterloo Massacre of Corn Law protestors 16 August	**1819**	Keats writes 'Ode to a Nightingale', 'The Eve of St Agnes', 'Ode on a Grecian Urn', 'La Belle dame sans Merci' and 'To Autumn'
Death of George III, Prince Regent succeeds as George IV	**1820**	Keats realises he is suffering from tuberculosis and travels to Rome
Start of Greek War of Independence (to 1827)	**1821**	Keats dies in Rome 23 February
	1822	Shelley drowns off the coast of Italy, 8 July
	1823	Byron goes to Greece to support the War of Independence
	1824	Byron dies in Missolonghi, Greece, 19 April
	1827	Blake dies 12 August
Death of George IV, succeeded by brother William III. Publication of *Rural Rides* by William Cobbett	**1830**	
Slavery is abolished in the British Empire	**1834**	Coleridge dies 25 July
Launch of S.S. *Great Britain* first iron-hulled ocean-going ship	**1843**	Wordsworth becomes Poet Laureate
	1850	Wordsworth dies 23 April; *The Prelude* is published posthumously

Index

Websites

http://www.wordsworth.org.uk
   (The Wordsworth Trust, Centre for British Romanticism)
http://www.keats-shelley-house.org/
   (Keats-Shelley House, Rome)
http://www.rc.umd.edu/indexjs.html
   (Romantic Circles ñ study of Romantic literature and culture)
http://heritage.virtualsite.co.uk/keats/assoc.html
   (Keats-Shelley Memorial Association, UK)
http://users.ox.ac.uk/~scat0385/
   (Romantics on the Net)

Places to visit

The Wordsworth Trust, Centre for British Romanticism, Dove Cottage, Grasmere, Cumbria LA22 9SH
   (tel: 015394 35544)
The Keats-Shelley Memorial House, 26 Piazza di Spagna, Rome, 00187, Italy (tel: (39) 06 678 4235)